**INDEX
BOOK**

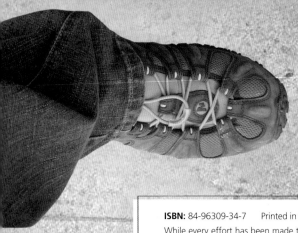

ISBN: 84-96309-34-7   Printed in China

SHAKE UP
YOUR IDEAS

T-Shirt 360* - Copyright / First Publication 2006
Publishing: Index Book SL. C/ Consell de Cent 160 local 3, 08015 Barcelona
Phone: +34 93 454 5547 **Fax:** +34 93 454 8438
E-mail: ib@indexbook.com **URL:** www.indexbook.com
Author/Graphic Design: Pedro Guitton
Illustration of the chapters: Guilherme Marconi **Translation:** Silvia Guiu
Printing: SNP Leefung Printers (Shenzhen) Co.,Ltd - SNP Leefung
Printing Building, No.1 Nangguang Road, Nanshan Zone, Shenzhen,P.R.C. - China
Tel: +86-755-86063923 **Fax:** +86-755-26644223 **E-mail:** minchao@snpcorp.com

Contents

PRINTING T-SHIRTS

People are often unreasonable, illogical, and self centered.
Forgive them anyway.
If you are kind, people may accuse you of selfish, ulterior motives.
Be kind anyway.
If you are successful, you will win some false friends and some true enemies.
Succeed anyway.
If you are honest and frank, people may cheat you.
Be honest and frank anyway.
What you spend years building someone could destroy over night.
Build anyway.
If you find serenity and happiness, they may be jealous
Be happy anyway.
The good you do today people will often forget tomorrow.
Do good anyway.
Give the world the best you have, and it may never be enough.
Give the world the best you've got anyway.
You see, in the final analysis, it is between you
and your individualism.
It was never between you and them anyway.

Be positive

Interview

We interviewed 6 people. Together, we shared good ideas about the market, reflecting on where we are now and the new directions we will take in the future.

after

Mutual
Response

HeadStrong

Accentuate
Clothing

Bonus T-Shirts

By the Booth

Bettino

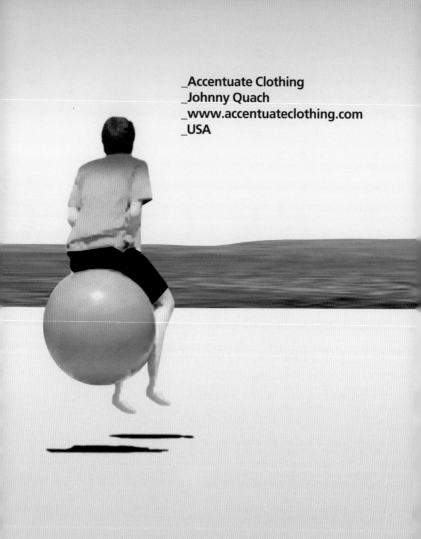

_Accentuate Clothing
_Johnny Quach
_www.accentuateclothing.com
_USA

- Describe Accentuate Clothing

Accentuate is essentially us making use of our talents to do what we enjoy and simultaneously attempt to make positive contributions. (To whom? It doesn't matter.) A wise man taught us the secret to sustained happiness is to figure out what you love doing and find a way to get paid for it. So here we are, giving all we've got, hoping to leave a good mark.

- How do you go about creating a new collection?

Our designs are representative of the collective inspirations we've amassed in life. We expound on the topics that we care about, and then give our best two cents in designing a cool T-shirt. Like any medium of art, sometimes it works and sometimes it doesn't, but we try to keep our critiques raw so we can have thoughtful products.

- What concepts is your target audience looking for?

Since we are new, it is difficult to say what it is exactly. However, we don't really stress over that. We are not as interested in pleasing everyone as we are in touching those who understand what we're about and love us for it. We like being loved.

- Do you work with a variety of materials or only special materials?

One of our first focuses is to make comfortable T-shirts. We don't mind the extra cost, because we feel this is our way of being loyal to our designs (as in, we don't want our pretty designs

printed onto cheap cloth). Once we get good at making comfortable shirts, we do plan to experiment with alternatives.

- What are the advantages and disadvantages of exclusivity and mass production?

It depends on for whom. ;) Exclusivity is nice, because it makes people feel special, but I personally am a fan of mass production. Most of the time, a mass produced product has a far greater voice in society. A clothing company is unlikely to ever have as much voice as an entertainment company, but at the same time probably more voice than mom-and-pop shops. And like I've said earlier, it would be nice if we could contribute something good to the world.

- Do you see the gay market as a potential market to be developed?

Maybe, but if the question is "would we act according to that?" then the answer is no. I'm not saying we don't care about making money, for money can do many things. But we believe that money is more of a byproduct rather than the purpose. As Jim Collins from Good to Great put it beautifully, "In a truly great company, profits and cash flow become like blood and water to a healthy body: They are absolutely essential for life, but they are not the very point of life."

As we continue to make clothes we believe to be beautiful, gays, straights, and others are all encouraged to fall in love with us.

salelations

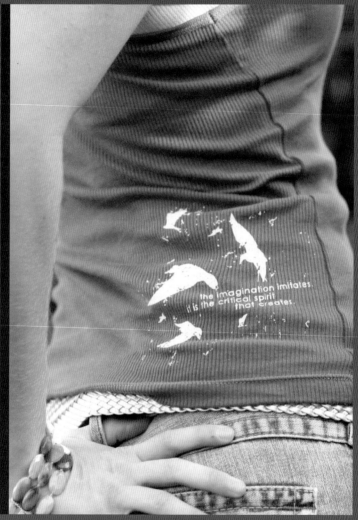

the imagination imitates.
it is the critical spirit
that creates.

Animals

the imagination ...tive.
It is the critical spirit
the creator.

001-002-003

Animals

Animals

FRIKI MITH XPERIENZIA
vegetais nunca mais!

007-008-009

Animals

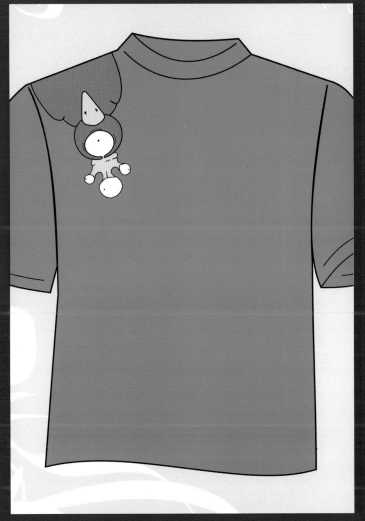

Animals

013-014-015

Animals

BONITO MS
1 | Amazona Aestiva
2 | Amazona Ochrocephala

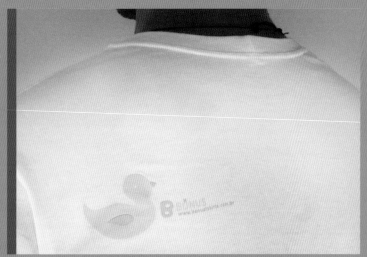

Animals

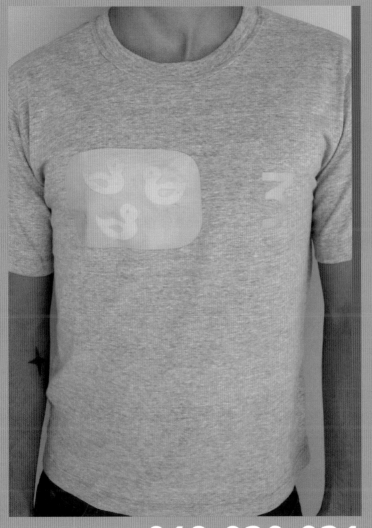

019-020-021

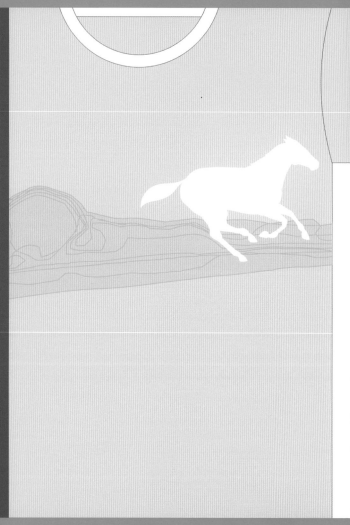

Animals

Animals

025-026-027

Animals

Animals

031-032-033

Animals

034-035-036

Animals

FIDALGO

037-038-039

l'Amante religieuse

"L'amante religieuse toujours va a la messe après un bon jeu de fesse.
Une fois expiée, elle rentre au foyer la conscience en paix "
(serigrafia. 2005)

Animals

040-041-042

Animals

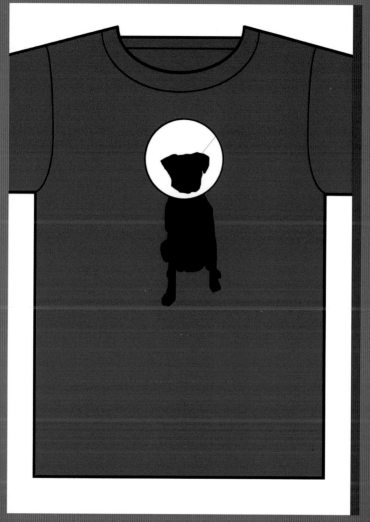

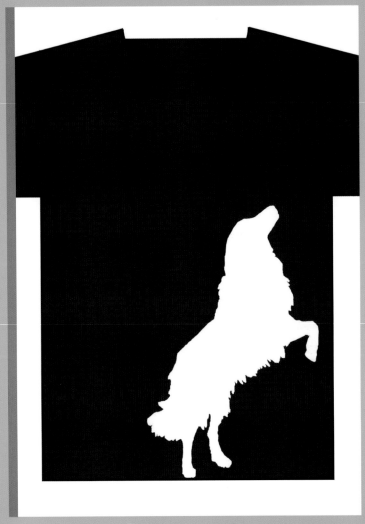

Animals

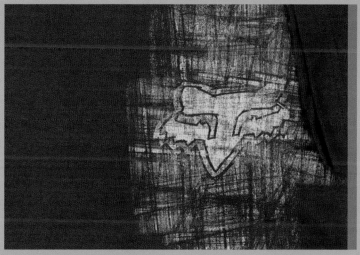

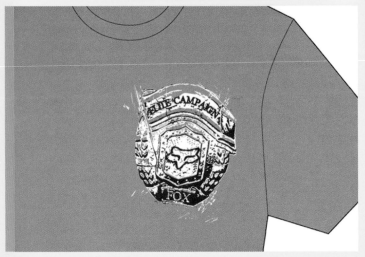

Animals

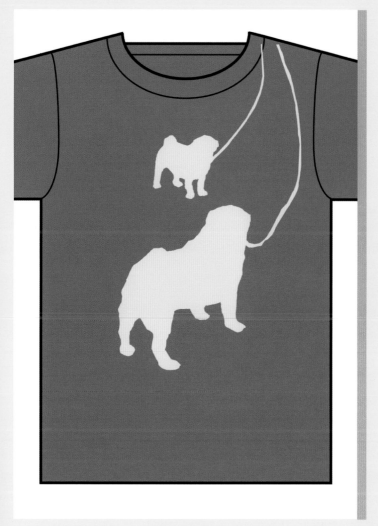

Animals

Animals

055-056-057

Animals

EM UMA REVOLUÇÃO SE TRIUNFA, OU SE MORRE....

Animals

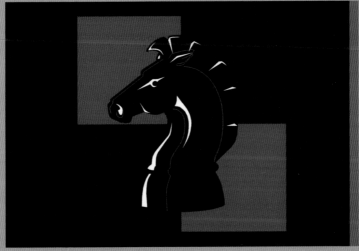

Animals

Josh Ritter

MEMORY
CAT

Animals

067-068-069

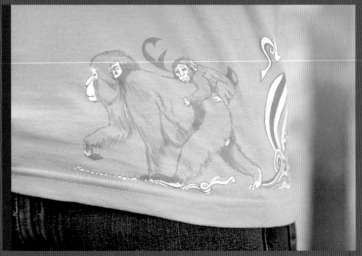

Animals

"I USED TO SWIM"

storyabout fish & suit

Animals

Animals

Les Coiseaux

"Quoi? tous ces oiseaux sont ils si sots que si tu
approches ils te découpent en morceaux
à coups de ciseaux "
(serigrafia. 2005)

Animals

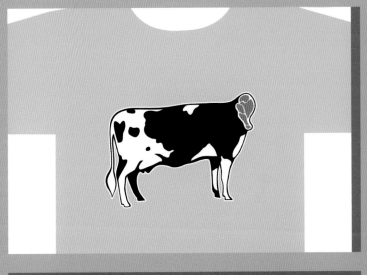

079-080-081

Animals

Animals

085-086-087

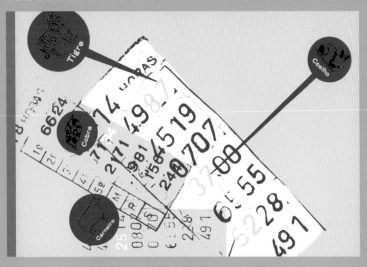

Animals

Animals

091_092_093

Animals

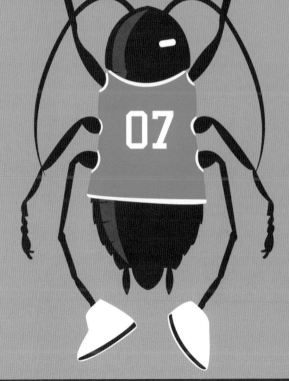

094-095-096

TOXI COW

Animals

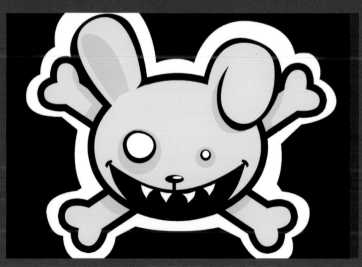

097_098_099

Animals

miau, miau

Animals

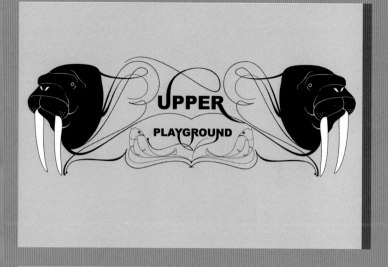

Animals

AMKA

SATANAS.DJ
AMKA

Animals

109-110-111

Animals

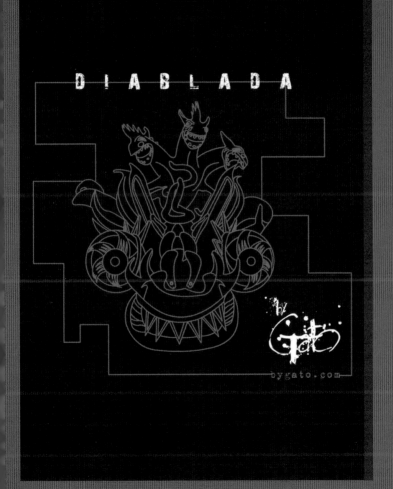

DIABLADA

by Gato
bygato.com

112-113-114

_Bettino
_Albert Carreras
_www.bettino.net
_Spain

- Is Barcelona a place of inspiration?
The city you live in affects you every morning when you get up. The sun and the Mediterranean always help to bring out ideas. In Barcelona, there are interesting things happening, such as the explosion of street art, but there is also a touch of boredom and general tedium. The city is a great observatory of everyday life and of what is happening in the rest of the world. You can always find input that will then turn into some new idea...

- What are the best ways to sell T-shirts?
Differentiation is one alternative. There are millions of T-shirts currently on sale in the shops. If you donít try to contribute something new, you have a difficult road ahead of you. You canít compete with the big brand names that sell T-shirts with a very low profit margin.

- What are the main advantages of new media?
In recent years, T-shirts have been rediscovered as a form of expression for the person wearing them. They act sort of like a person's individual call, an attempt to differentiate themselves from the rest of the masses. Another possibility is that of the human ad sponsored by a brand name. And of course, they are totally comfortable and have a wide range of colors to combine with.

- Why are T-shirts present in all social classes?
Because they are comfortable and because they are easy to combine with other garments that

can make them a synonym of elegance. Yet, at the same time, they can also be a sign of informality. Because they become a banner of a personís unique personality. Because they are reasonably priced, in general... They're like jeans which have become popular classics.

- What are the main techniques used in making T-shirts?
From silkscreen printing and transfer to customization... Anything can be used to give expression to an idea.

- What are the advantages and disadvantages of exclusivity and mass production?
Exclusivity gives you more creative liberty. The people that wear your clothes know that that what they are wearing is unique and that they are not going to see it in large chain stores. On the other hand, sales are lower and finding new markets and distribution is complicated business. In large-scale sales, production is higher, costs lower, profits greater, but you risk potentially losing control in some fields.

- What kind of message do you transmit in your creations?
We are trying to achieve a sort of smiley, fun, a concept, ideas, trying to take things out of their natural habitat, mix them up so that the result is as close as you can get to foolishness. We don't believe in illustration for illustration's sake, and we don't believe in prettiness. As I said before, there are too many T-shirts in the market to stand out with an illustration that has nothing behind it.

sex Jokes

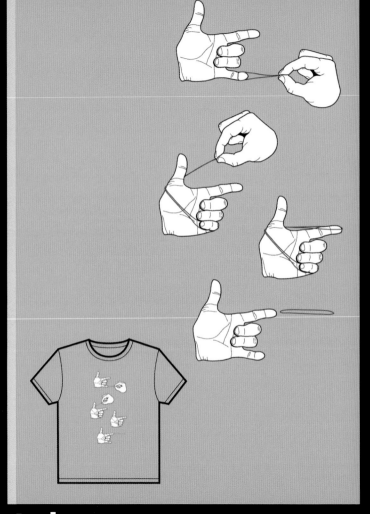

Jokes

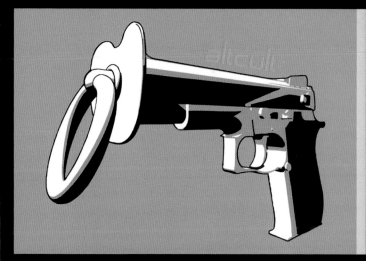

115-116-117

Jokes

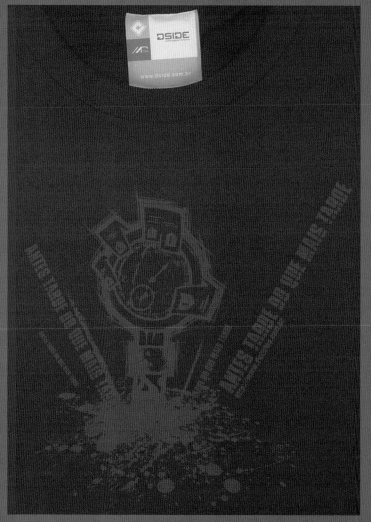

Jokes

100% IMPERFECT

130-131-132

Jokes

forgiven

YOU ARE THE MOST
BEAUTIFUL

133-134-135

AVOID
EYE CONTACT

SINGLE

136-137-138

PORQUE
YO LO
BALGO!

Jokes

SELFISH
IN BED

NOT FOR SALE

139-140-141

Jokes

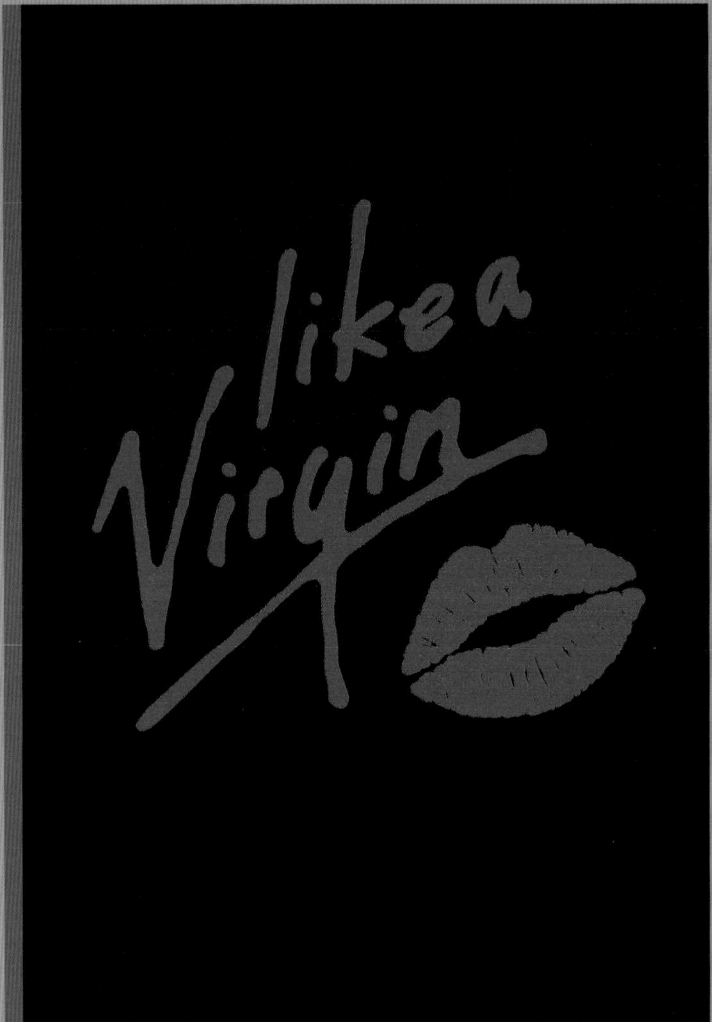

Jokes

¡MOLA!

BVLGAR

Jokes

chicca

Jokes

151-152-153

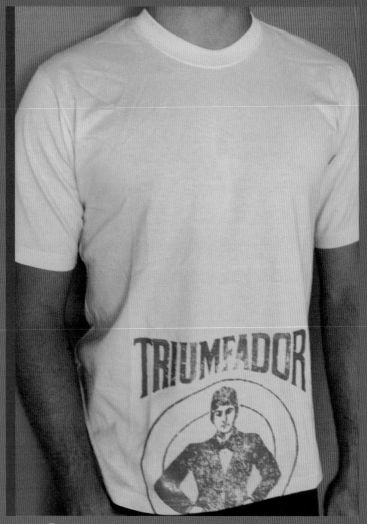

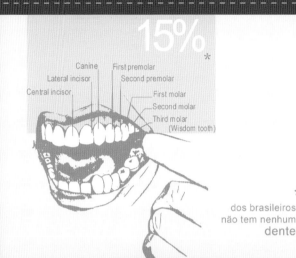

15%*

Canine · First premolar
Lateral incisor · Second premolar
Central incisor · First molar
· Second molar
· Third molar
(Wisdom tooth)

*

dos brasileiros
não tem nenhum
dente

Jokes

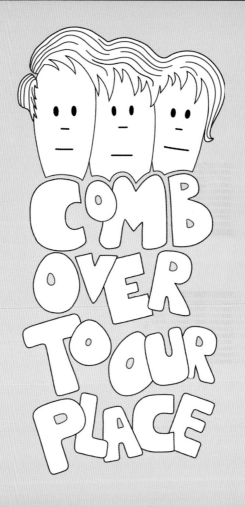

157-158-159

Heavy
Rotation

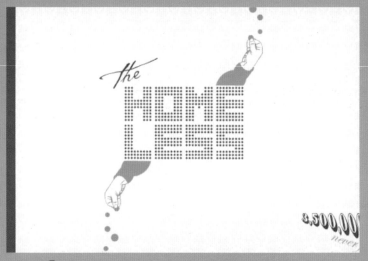

Jokes

Jokes

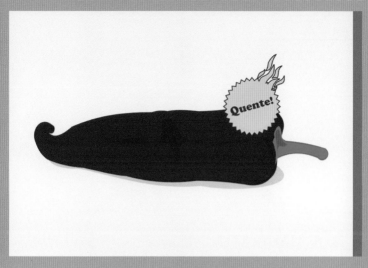

.Jokes

Jokes

Jokes

DESTROY HIM, MY ROBOTS.

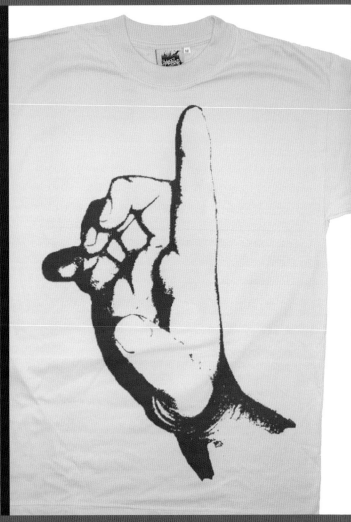

Jokes

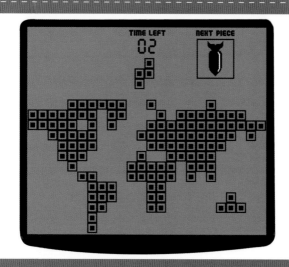

184-185-186

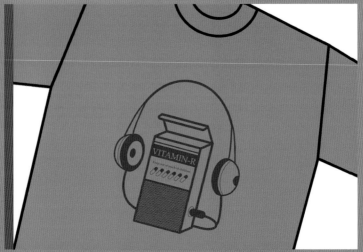

Jokes

GAME OVER

Jokes

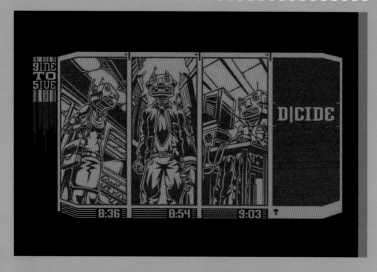

Jokes

193_194_195

Jokes

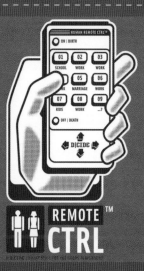

.Jokes

199-200-201

Jokes

Jokes

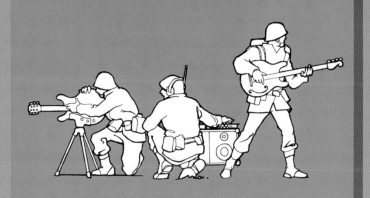

Jokes

Jokes

211-212-213

SPAGHETTI VILLE

Jokes

SE✕BLO®

THE SUBURBAN SEX BLOG

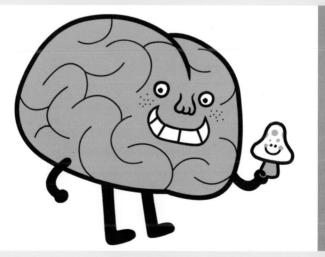

217-218-219

.Jokes

220-221-222

223-224-2

La machine à coudre

Jokes

226-227-228

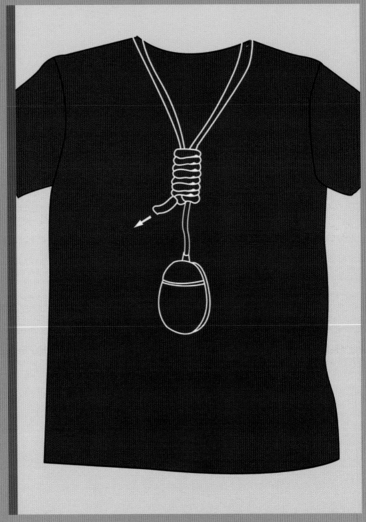

Jokes

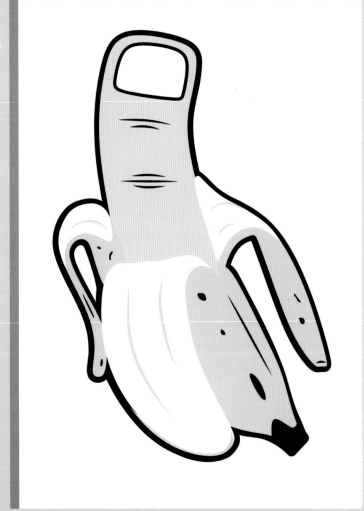

Jokes

235-236-237

FLYING IDEAS

LESS ONE CAR

Jokes

REVENGE
OF THE
DEER

Jokes

ANTI - WAR F.C.

السلام

للعالم

WORLD PEACE

SEXBOMB

241-242-243

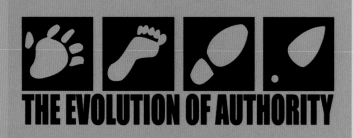

THE EVOLUTION OF AUTHORITY

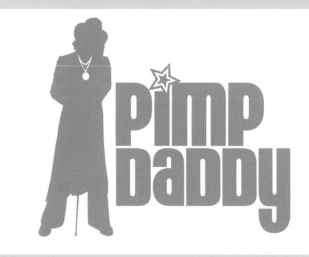

Jokes

iJesus

TRUE LOVE

STUDENT

247-248-249

BUCK FUSH

MO' WAR!

Jokes

_Bonus T-Shirts
_Renato Japiassú "Japi"
_www.bonustshirts.com.br
_Brazil

- How long have you been working in this field?

I've been working with T-shirts for three years. When I started, I was not satisfied with the T-shirts available in the market and their prices. I felt that they didn't represent me, and honestly speaking, T-shirts are a fantastic vehicle for personal expression. There's nothing more personal than developing stamps with the images that live in my head, and why not put them on my chest and back?

- How do you go about creating a new collection?

For me, the process is really similar to creating art. It's very intuitive and experimentalist. It is an attempt to find a creative essence that is unique and personal and honest—because the people that buy designs feel that honesty—and that incorporates subconscious symbols. Wearers identify with such images, and

that is the magic of creation: using exactly those symbols which represent something personal, something individual. People form their own mosaics with images and attribute meanings. They feel a sense of pride in their T-shirts as a type of open reflection of their ideas and sensitivity.

- What is the future of this field?

Good. I think that this field will tend to grow exponentially along with all the other fields that are working to come closer and closer to the consumer. It is clear that in a mass society like ours, where the need to affirm our own individual identity is ever more present, everything will tend to adapt to us, giving us the sense of finding, in the art of a product, that it was made just for us and that it represents us in a variety of ways. In this sense, T-shirts have been very successful, because they are a product at a price that is accessible and with many production possibilities, ranging from industrial to at-home production without requiring large production runs.

- What are the most creative ways to sell T-shirts?

Ways that explore interactive methods, where the T-shirts pass through a series of virtual contests to see which are selected as the best. This method is already is already wide-spread, because this is the only way that people can interact with the creation before it is produced. Many people import T-shirts, since symbols from other countries seem much more exotic when compared with the local culture, differentiating the consumer from other people still more. In reality, the possibilities are infinite. The product does not take up much space, does not weigh much and

can be presented in many different ways. The methods for selling them are innumerable, and the packaging and possible accessories are also countless.

- Why are T-shirts present in all social classes?

They are a product that is cheap, comfortable and has grand communicative power. The symbols, aesthetics, quality of fabric, model, finishing touches, etc. all change, but the basic concept is the same for everyone—not just for all social classes, but also for all ages and both sexes. The number of women wearing T-shirts is increasing significantly.

- What are the main techniques used in making T-shirts?

99% of the T-shirts are made by silkscreen. There is a hot stamp used for images with foil and a whole world of other effects done by hand, such as embroidery, match work, tie-dye and many others. At the moment, for silk screening, there are techniques like silicone, foie, puff, high relief, plasta sol, etc.

- What is the relationship between fashion, art and design?

Wardrobes have existed since the beginning of time. Art explores individuality, and design works in mass communication.

- What are the attributes necessary for a brand to stand out in the market?

That depends on the market. There are markets where more mass production is better. Others focus on exclusivity. The brand has to be very clear on what its target audience is and what return it expects to generate. Focusing on this, it must try to differentiate itself in a positive way. This is the conservative bit of advice. The personal one is to be true to your intuition and your creativity. Your followers will appear if you really do have talent.

miscellany

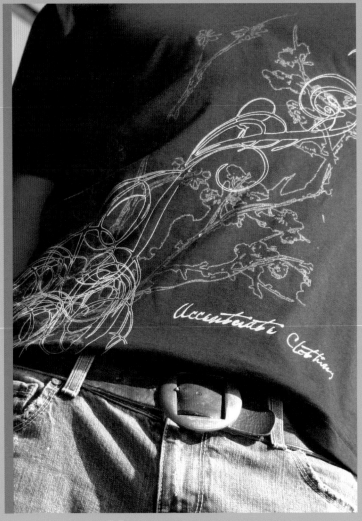

Miscellany

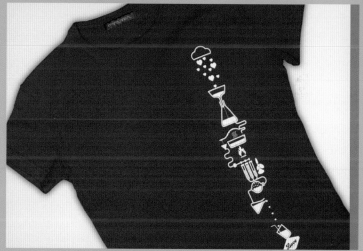

Miscellany

259-260-261

Miscellany

262-263-264

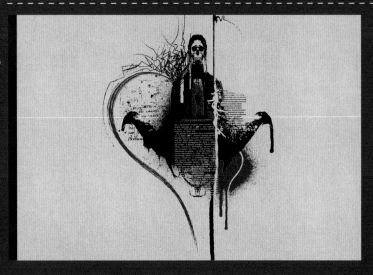

Miscellany

265-266-267

Miscellany

Miscellany

REFEN.SKATEBOARDS
SUPPORTING THE UNDERGROUND CULTURE

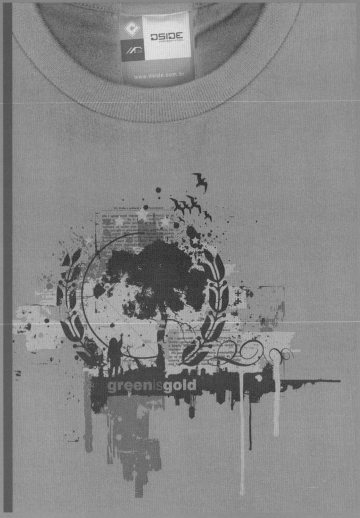

Miscellany

BONITO MS

Miscellany

BONITO MS

277-278-279

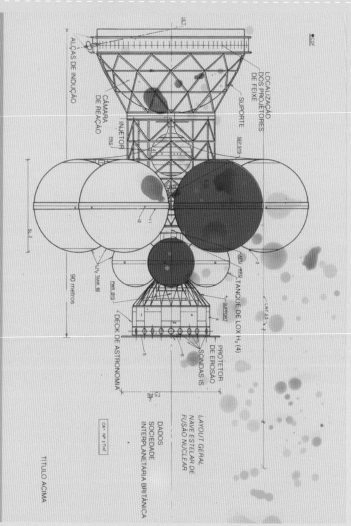

ALÇAS DE INDUÇÃO

LOCALIZAÇÃO
DOS PROJETORES
DE FEIXE

CÂMARA
DE REAÇÃO

SUPORTE

INJETOR

TANQUE DE LOX H₂ (4)

90 metros

PROTETOR
DE EROSÃO

DECK DE ASTRONOMIA

SONDAS IS

LAYOUT GERAL
NAVE ESTELAR DE
FUSÃO NUCLEAR

DADOS
SOCIEDADE
INTERPLANETÁRIA BRITÂNICA

TÍTULO ACIMA

Miscellany

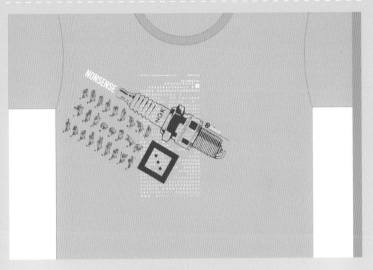

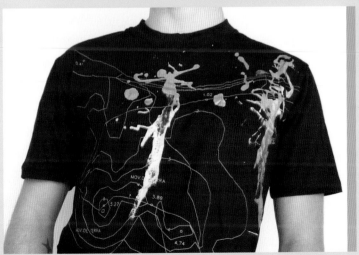

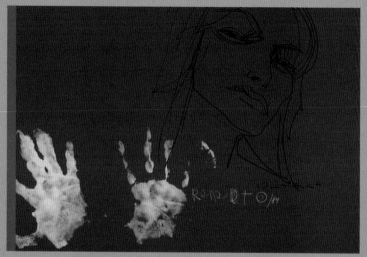

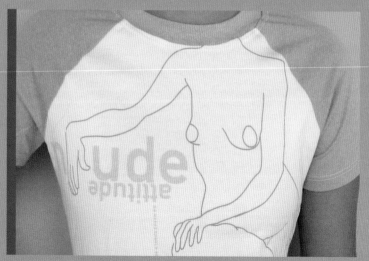

Miscellany

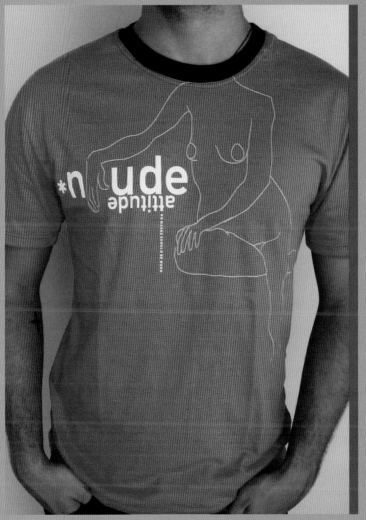

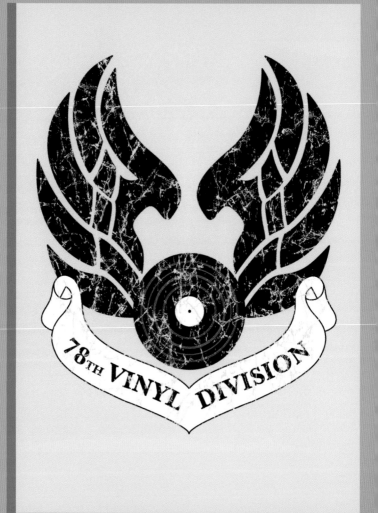

Miscellany

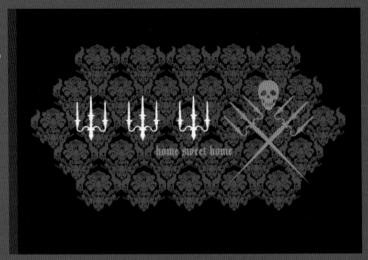

Miscellany

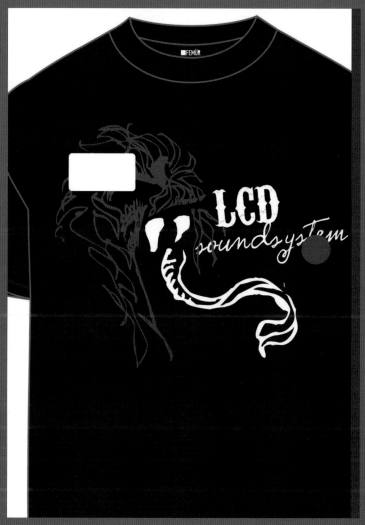

Miscellany

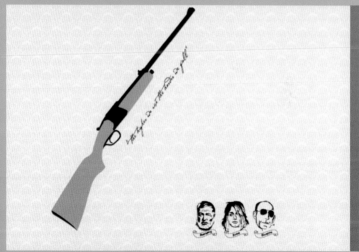

292-293-294

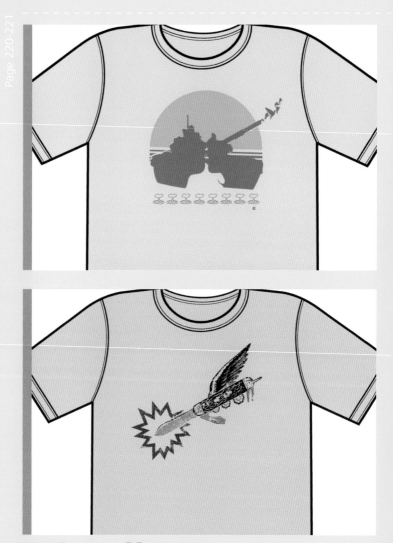

Miscellany

Miscellany

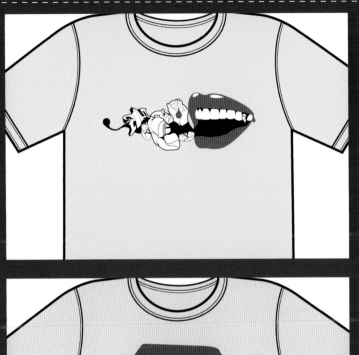

BROKE MY KEISTER
AT CHICHEN ITZA

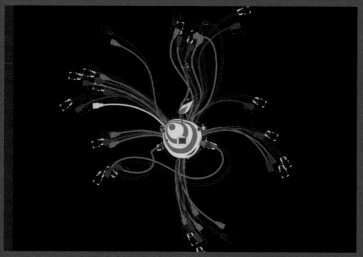

Miscellany

headstrong

304-305-306

Miscellany

307-308-309

Miscellany

310_311_312

Miscellany

313_314_315

Miscellany

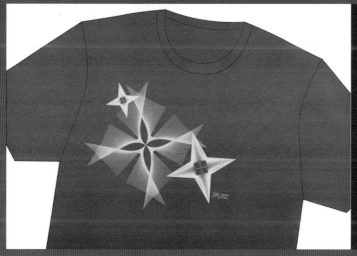

316-317-318

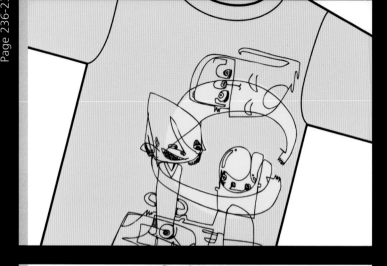

Miscellany

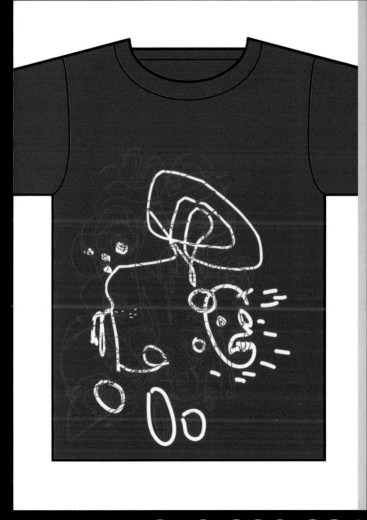

319-320-321

Miscellany

Miscellany

325-326-327

ENTREGUE SUAS ARMAS...
NUNCA DESISTA DOS SEUS IDEAIS..

EM UMA REVOLUÇÃO SE TRIUNFA,
OU SE MORRE.....

Miscellany

Miscellany

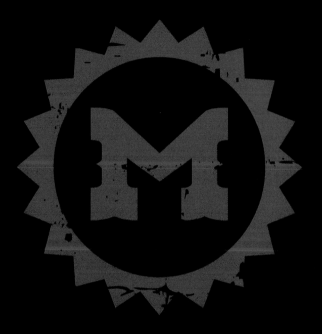

MARGINALE.COM

JARDIM OPERÁRIO
FOOTBALL CLUB

VÁRZEA
LEAGUE

Miscellany

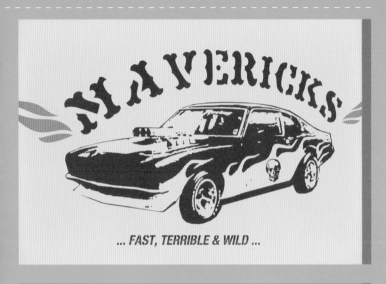

... FAST, TERRIBLE & WILD ...

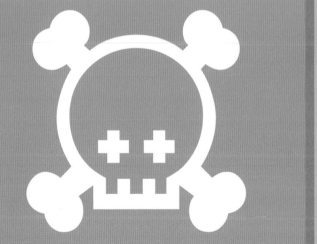

334-335-336

Miscellany

337-338-339

Miscellany

Miscellany

343-344-345

Miscellany

346-347-348

Miscellany

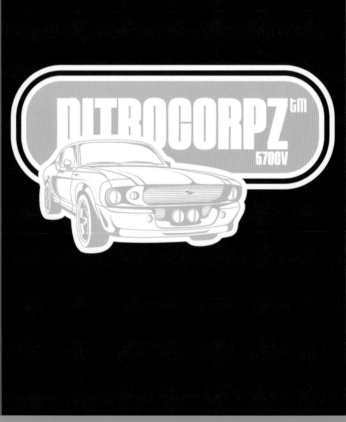

Miscellany

Miscellany

355-356-357

Miscellany

Miscellany

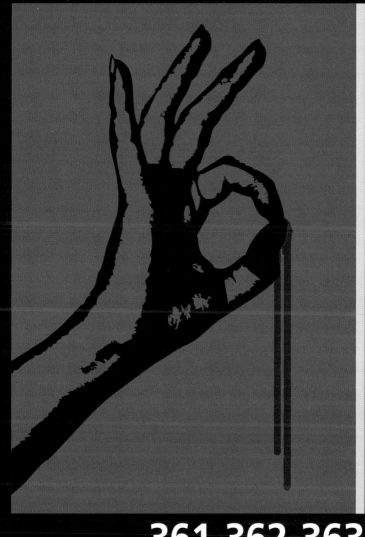

361-362-363

MEATSHAKE
*existe en version volail
et dans tout les groupes sanguins

SANS
OGM

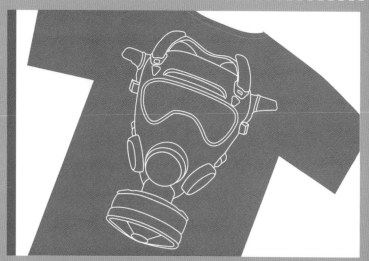

Miscellany

367-368-369

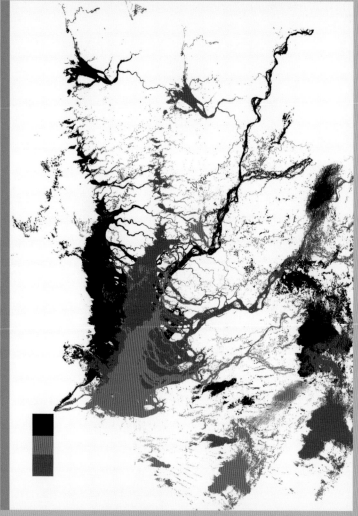

Miscellany

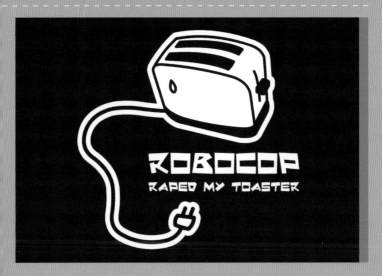

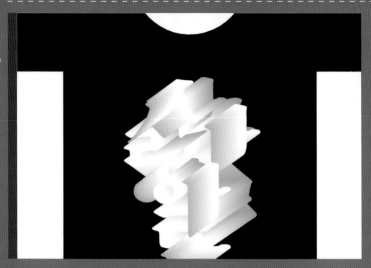

Miscellany

Miscellany

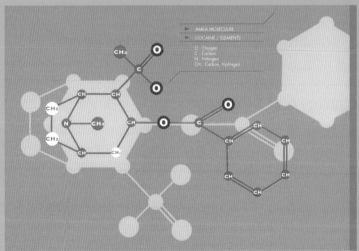

AMKA MOLECULAR

COCAINE / ELEMENTS

O : Oxygen
C : Carbon
N : Nitrogen
CH : Carbon, Hydrogen

Miscellany

379.380.381

Miscellany

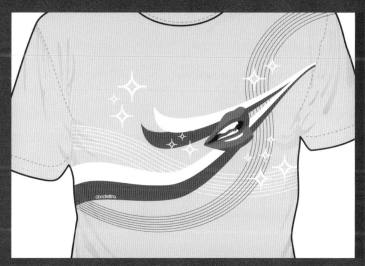

Miscellany

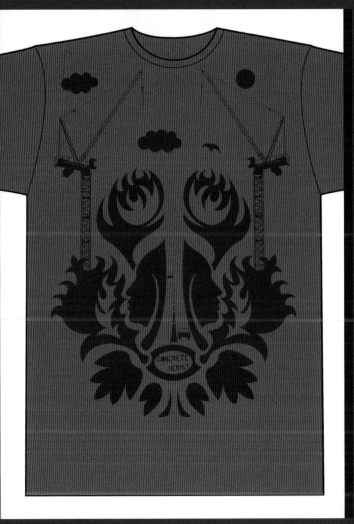

385-386-387

FOLD AND PLAY series 2/3: ROBOTO-808
Arts and Crafts Action Figure Playset

ORIGAMI
ATTACK

Miscellany

388_389_390

_By the Booth
_Garus Booth
_www.bythebooth.com
_Canada

- Is Canada a place of inspiration?
I would have to say yes. Canada in relation to the rest of the world is both a guest and a gracious host. This mingling of cultures and ideas creates a dynamic working environment. Something about this breeds creativity.

- Describe bythebooth.
bythebooth was conceived at the beginning of this year, 2005. It is a multidisciplinary boutique firm. bythebooth is about personality, finding the simple and powerful nuances that set each client apart, then taking those special moments and displaying them as essential qualities.

- What makes your T-shirts different?
Our shirts along with all bythebooth products are a direct result of our work, in that they showcase the personal expression that drives the work. Our products are printed in limited runs making each piece unique.

- Do you have any commercial restrictions that limit creativity?
I never work with any sort of restriction. If I am feeling the design and would rock it myself, then I have no problem producing it. Design is about pushing and bending limits.

- What are the most important components for a T-shirt to be accepted in the market?
A shirt has to be comfortable above anything. I am extremely particular about fit. You have to have the thing on all day. As far as graphics, the shirt, like any good design, must have a strong concept, and it must reflect the individual ideology of the consumer.

People

People

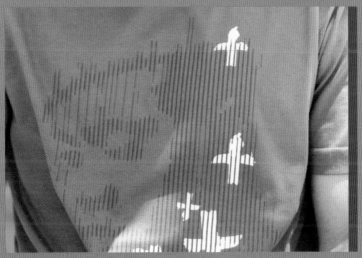

People

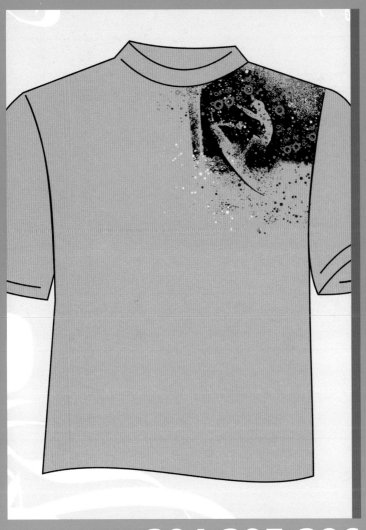

394_395_396

People

397_398_399

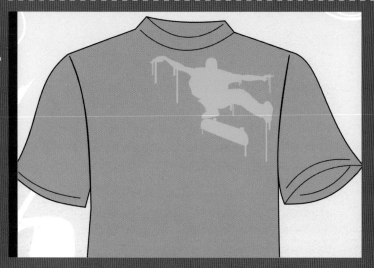

People

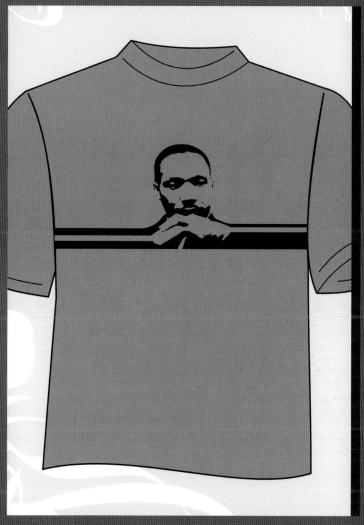

400-401-402

People

403-404-405

People

UBIRAJARA

People

409-410-411

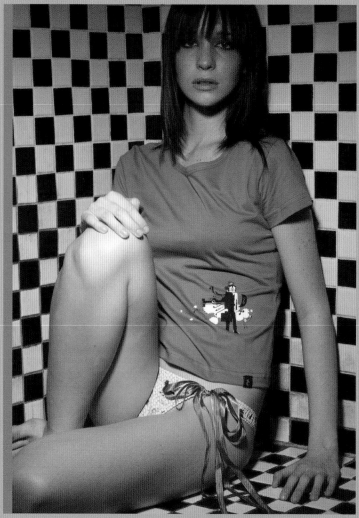

People

412-413-414

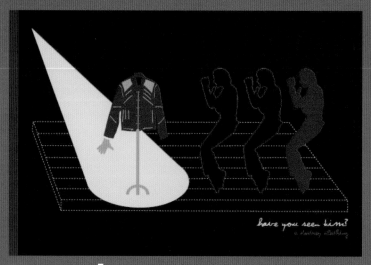

have you seen him?
a darkwing clothing

People

415-416-417

People

418-419-420

...what are friends for?

People

Je te Touche

"Gare à celui qui touche la touche qui fait mouche"

(serigrafia. 2004)

421-422-423

People

PARANOIA
PARANOIA
PARANOIA
PARANOIA

424-425-426

People

People

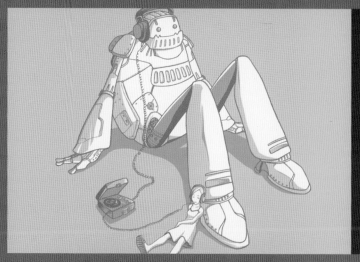

430-431-432

People

433-434-435

People

People

439-440-441

People

442-443-444

People

445-446-447

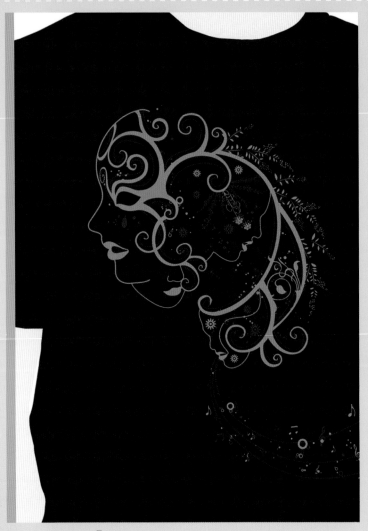

People

People

People

454-455-456

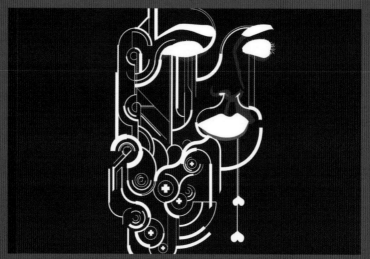

People

People

460-461-462

People

463-464-465

head strong

People

466-467-468

People

469-470-471

People

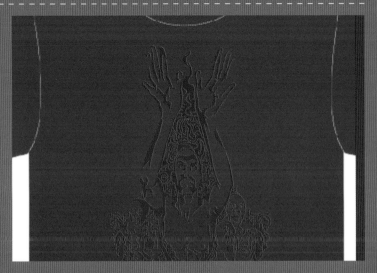

472-473-474

People

475-476-477

Peace Off

"Peace asi... Pues sinceramente,
no se yo si voy a seguir aqui..."
(serigrafia. 2005)

People

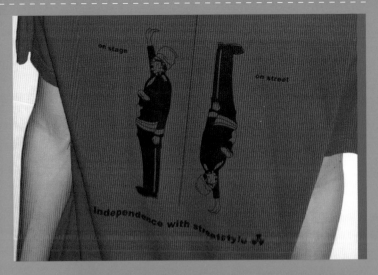

black4ever

People

481-482-483

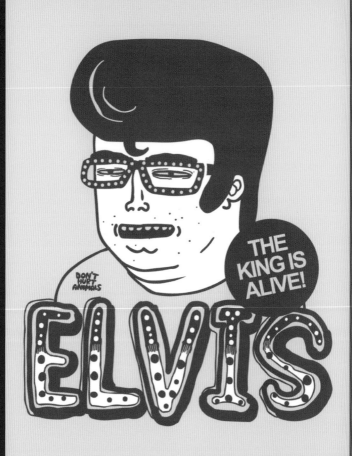

People

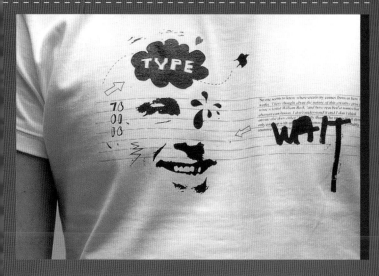

People

487-488-489

People

490-491-492

People

493-494-495

Roots

496-497-498

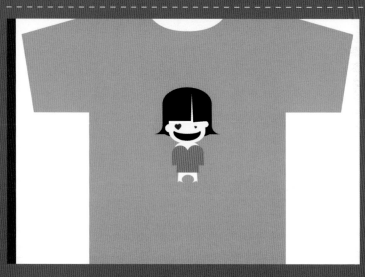

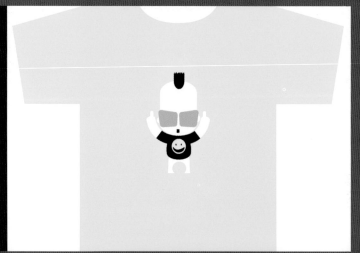

People

499_500_501

People

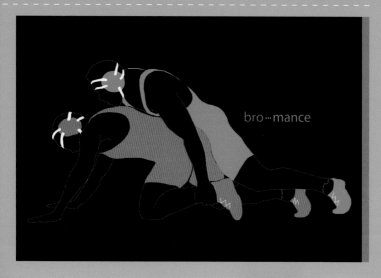

bro⋯mance

People

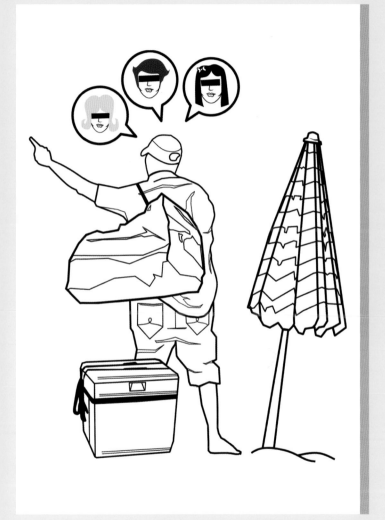

505-506-507

People

508-509-510

People

People

EL DIEGO

514-515-516

People

517·518·519

People

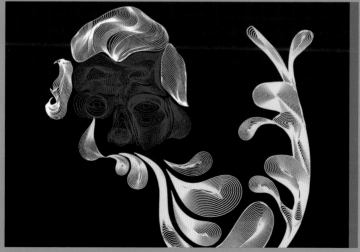

520-521-522

_HeadStrong
_Glyn Berrington
_www.headstrong.co.uk
_London

- Is London a place of inspiration?

Not for me. When I was 15 or 16, I used to hang around King's Road and the music venues of London, but I never lived there or anywhere near. Nowadays, I live in the countryside and find inspiration from many walks of life.

- Describe HeadStrong.

"It's me" is the easy answer. It's my life, and it's about my life and experiences. Other than that, it's an online shop that sells clothes that I like.

- Do you only work online or do you also have a shop? What are the main advantages and disadvantages?

We are only online since 1999. There are many advantages and disadvantages of both, but you just have to make the most of what you do. For us, personally, we never try to do what has been done before, so we continually look for ways to be original or at least to bring new ideas to different groups.

- Where do you find your inspiration?

It's not fair to say it's all me, because I have the easy bit. I see designs or designers that I like, and I approach them to do a design for us. Having said that, I never put constraints on designers and turn down many designs that I think are not the style of the designer. Let me explain. I approach designers because I like their work and usually because it's different, but sometimes they try and do a headstrong design that is not what we are about. It's about designs I like and designers doing their own thing.

- Who has designed for HeadStrong?

Well, our oldest friend has to be Frame/Framer/Leeframer. The guy is a genius and has done work for HeadStrong for years. He has worked as designer for many magazines, including Graffiti and Music, but designs for a few big international clothing companies. We are very lucky that he feels what we are doing, and we work together whenever possible. I would like to call all the designers that have done work for us friends, and I regularly get asked by companies if I could supply designers, which I do but never take anything for myself, since it's just helping friends. Shouts to designers who have helped us, in no order: Cheba, Eco, Kid Acne, Rough, Sickboy.

- What is the biggest challenge when developing a print?

Trying do something different in a very worked-out medium, but generally it's cutting colors down and producing artwork that everybody is happy with.

- Think of one of your T-shirts that sold out. Why was it such a success?

Because people liked it or felt what we were trying to do at that time.

Blaces

MADE IN ⚙ BRAZIL

Places

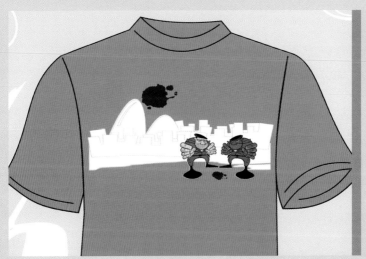

523-524-525

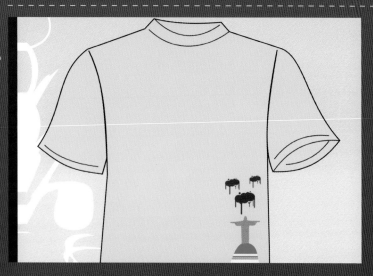

Places

526-527-528

Places

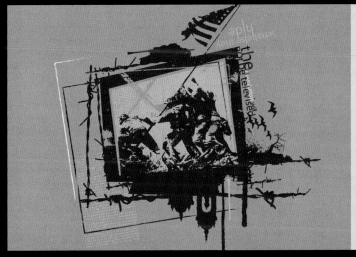

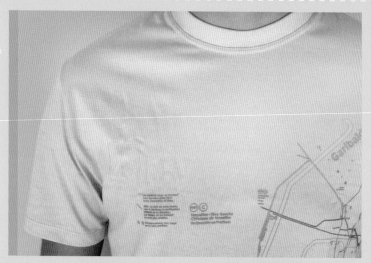

Places

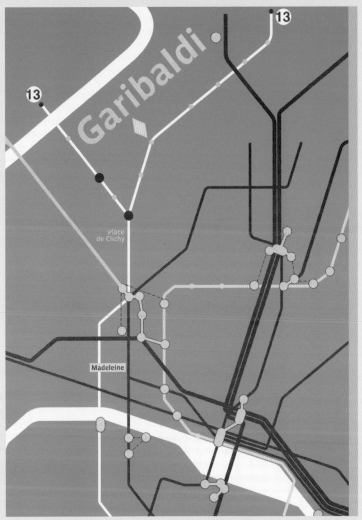

International League

BOGOTA

Traffics

Places

Places

Cuba
*
La Isla

538-539-540

Places

541-542-543

Places

544-545-546

LEGALIZE CANADA!

Places

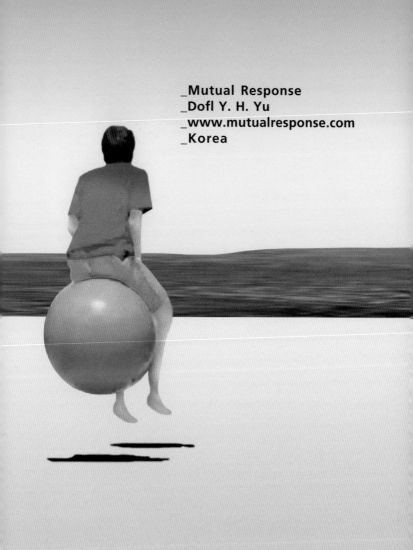

_Mutual Response
_Dofl Y. H. Yu
_www.mutualresponse.com
_Korea

- **Is Hong Kong a place of inspiration?**

Yes, sure. This is an international city, so I can meet many people with different cultures. If you walk down this street for a few minutes, then you will agree with me. I have been living in Hong Kong for about 4 years , and I have had many inspiring experiences.

- **What is the difference between Western and Eastern styles when talking about the creation and development of a concept? Do you have a special way of treating this difference?**

I don't prefer one specific thing. I just try to choose the best way to express the subject for every project. I am a young designer, so I still want to try many styles ranging from Eastern and Western. That means that sometimes I try Eastern, sometimes Western, and sometimes a mixture of both styles.

- **How did you get the ideas for your collections?**

I've always been interested in designing T-shirts, so it was a good opportunity for me to participate. I was interested in creating randomly generated images, so I generated some

random shapes in flash, which then I took and put on my T-shirts.

- **What do your T-shirts transmit that others do not?**

Although fractal patterns seem chaotic and unorganized, they consist of rules and formulas. By using a generating engine, an image that can never be recreated, will be produced using fractal rules.

- **Do you see children as a potential T-shirt market?**

Children are more naïve than adults, and they don't have biases. They act on visual design in an easy way, so there are other better potential T-shirt markets.

- **Any trips for people just starting?**

I have been working as a designer for about 5 years, but I just started in T-shirt design. If I can tell you one thing, then I'll tell you this: "Don't follow the designs of other designers, and try to show your own colors. This is not only true for T-shirts but for design in general."

txB88graphy

...and you will
find out
how to unfold
our wings
as you fall...

Typography

550-551-552

Typography

553-554-555

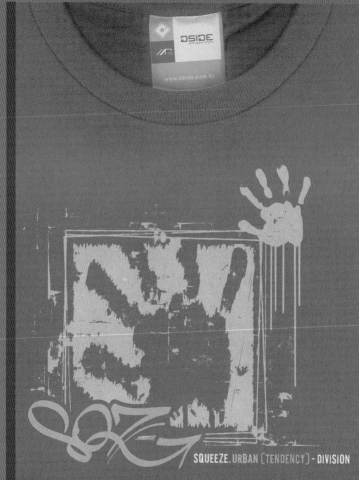

SQUEEZE. URBAN (TENDENCY) - DIVISION

Typography

556-557-558

Typography

Death to Digital

559-560-561

Typography

562-563-564

Typography

565-566-567

Typography

568-569-570

bythebooth.com

Typography

574-575-576

MISCHIEF
SKATE STORE
EST1996TEESSIDE

Typography

577-578-579

Van der Dürke

Typography

580-581-582

Typography

583-584-585

Typography

586-587-588

Typography

589-590-591

Typography

592-593-594

Typography

3TT LA VIE EN ROSE
(mixed media 2004)

Typography

598-599-600

Typography

601-602-603

Typography

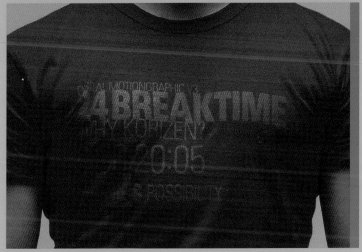

Typography

607-608-609

Typography

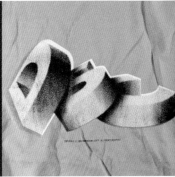

Directory
by name

--- Accentuate - johnny@accentuateclothing.com
001, 002, 256, 257, 261, 392, 393, 550

--- Akafab - stuff@akafab.com
003, 004, 115, 116, 394

--- Alternateev shop - alternateev@hotmail.com
607

--- Altcult - altlink@altcult.com
117

--- Amkashop - info@amkashop.com
108, 109, 110, 112, 113, 376, 378, 381, 628, 630, 633

--- Anton Repponen - anton_repponen@hotmail.com
118, 258, 395

--- Arnwa - ronald@arnwa.com
379, 519

--- Artur Kja - guerrilha.ct@gmail.com
005, 008, 009, 010, 011, 012, 013, 119, 120, 121, 122, 123, 124, 125, 126, 128,
259, 260, 262, 263, 267, 391, 396, 397, 398, 399, 400, 402, 403, 525, 526, 527

--- Atnic - nina@stalina.de
015

--- Atypyk – contact@atypyk.com
129, 130, 131, 134, 135, 136, 137, 140, 141, 142, 143, 146

--- Augusto Reis – contact@dside.com.br
127, 132, 264, 265, 268, 269, 273, 274, 401, 404, 417, 530, 531, 555, 556

--- Auslander - contato@auslander.com.br
380

--- Balcony-ppl - visualmorphers@yahoo.com
266, 270, 271, 272, 275, 276, 277, 405, 409, 410

--- beMyself - mcroura@hotmail.com
111, 253, 382

--- beneltonjohn - info@beneltonjohn.com
114, 631

--- Bettino - beto@beto-caracas.jazztel.es
006, 133, 138, 139, 144, 145, 147, 148, 149, 150, 151, 152,
153, 406

--- boboswear - info@boboswear.it
517

--- Bonus T-Shirts - renatojapi@hotmail.com
016, 017, 018, 019, 021, 022, 154, 155, 278, 279, 280, 281,
282, 283, 284, 285, 532, 534

--- Booware - us@boohome.com
023, 024, 287

--- Breadson - paolo.valzania@virgilio.it
383, 632

--- Brian Kroeker - hello@briankroeker.com
255

--- By Gato - bygato@gmail.com
114

--- Camiseteria - info@camiseteria.com.br
156, 157, 407, 408, 412, 413, 474

--- Carlos Cañellas - carles@batllegroup.com
288, 551

--- Clandestina - pmirra@terra.com.br
384

--- Coletanea - guto@coletanea.art.br
390

--- Concrete Hermit - info@concretehermit.com
387

--- Cotton and Canvas - orders@cottonandcanvas.com
518

--- Dale Murray - dale@itchcom.com
158, 159, 160, 161, 162, 286, 414, 552, 561

--- David Steel - info@whoisdavidsteel.com
025, 027, 028, 411, 415

--- Destroy Clothing - adam@destroyclothing.com
163, 164, 289, 290, 293, 294, 301, 416, 419, 420, 421, 422,
425, 426, 427, 533, 536, 553, 554, 557, 558, 559, 560

--- Destructed - philipp@destructed.info
385

--- Dimension 7 - crew@dimension7.ch
611, 612

--- Distritozero - 3ttman@distritozero.com
14, 40, 79, 113, 386, 423, 478, 509, 597

--- Eduardo Duccigne - eduardo@ilusorium.net
020, 026, 166, 167, 428, 429, 563

--- Edward Stuart - e_c_stuart@hotmail.com
437, 562, 564

--- Esa Peltonen - esa.peltonen@9cm.net
388

--- Elshopo - jer@elshopo.com
565

--- Embassy - victor@aurabarcelona.com
029, 030, 033, 034, 045, 292, 295, 296, 299, 300, 418, 424, 430,
432

--- Endlessway - nikita@entity.ee
031, 297, 302, 305, 306

--- Fabio Nakane - fnakane@yahoo.com.br
433, 434, 435

--- Femur - info@femur.com.br
168, 169, 170, 291, 436, 438, 441

--- Fidalgo - contato@marcioismail.com.br
039, 165, 171, 566, 569, 570

--- Fonkyphi - phil.lihp@gmail.com
389

--- Garus Booth - bythebooth@bythebooth.com
173, 174, 175, 307, 571, 575

--- Gary Gao - angrytoast@gmail.com
431, 439

--- Goodforhealth - info@goodforhealth.tk
176

--- Guilherme Marconi - marconi@cloning.com.br
037, 038, 177, 179, 181, 182, 308, 309, 440, 442, 443, 444, 445, 446, 447, 448, 449, 453, 454, 459, 460, 528, 529, 538

--- Gustavo Machado - gustavo@gustavo-machado.com
608

--- Harderthansatan - info@harderthansatan.com
450, 451

--- Haroldo Portella - hportela@iis.com.br
180, 311, 312, 452, 455, 456, 572

--- Hayato Kamono - hayatok@designurge.com
185, 457, 458

--- Headstrong - info@headstrong.co.uk
172, 178, 183, 184, 186, 298, 303, 304, 313, 461, 462, 464, 465, 466, 469, 471, 567, 568, 573, 624

--- Hugo Mulder - dhm@euronet.nl
032, 035, 036, 041, 042, 043, 044, 047, 463, 467, 468, 576

--- Hype Type Studio - paul@hypetype.co.uk
048, 049, 050, 053, 054, 310, 314, 315, 316, 317, 318, 320, 577, 578, 587, 588, 589, 590, 593, 594

--- ilovesideline - james@ilovesideline.com
046, 051, 319, 321, 323

--- Jaguar Negro - info@jaguar-negro.com
052, 063, 189

--- Jason Byron Nelson - info@jasonbyronnelson.com
470, 472, 473

--- John Wingard Design - jw@johnwingarddesign.com
574

--- Jujuba Preta - info@tiagoteixeira.com.br
056, 475, 483

--- Khimaira - khimairaproject@free.fr
203

--- Koagfx - koadzn@club-internet.fr
324, 325, 326

--- Kraftmedia - info@kraftmedia.com
524

--- Lalacompany - info@lalacompany.com
059, 187, 188, 329, 479

--- Lars Niebuhr - lars@dcidenow.com
191, 192, 193, 194, 197, 198, 480, 595

--- Leo Uzai - leo.uzai@gmail.com
330

--- Licoszen - zenlicos@hotmail.com
520

--- Lowriderteeshirt - shop@lowriderteeshirt.ch
055, 057, 058, 190, 195, 322, 327, 331, 332, 579, 581,
582, 583, 584

--- Luciano Cian Van Der Durke - cian@hiatofc.com.br
060, 062, 196, 199, 200, 328, 333, 334, 335, 336, 337, 481, 482,
523, 535, 539, 540, 580, 585

--- MAKI ontwerp en illustratie - ontwerpenillustratie@yahoo.com
061, 064, 065, 201, 202, 204, 338, 339, 586, 591, 592, 599, 600

--- Matthew Fleming - matthew@blackt-shirt.com
066, 207, 477, 598

--- Mauro Gatti - mauro_brain@hotmail.com
205, 206, 208, 209, 210, 211, 212, 213, 214, 215, 216, 218,
219, 220, 221, 223, 228, 484

--- Monsieurt - monsieurt@totinette.com
068, 069, 070, 071, 074, 224, 225, 226, 227, 340, 341, 342,
343, 344, 347, 348, 349, 601

--- Mutual Response - contact@mutualresponse.com
067, 072, 345, 350, 351, 353, 354, 485, 486, 487, 488, 489,
490, 491, 492, 495, 602, 603, 605, 606

--- Nico / SKGZ - skgz@free.fr
112

--- Nitrocorpz - marck@nitrocorpz.com
075, 076, 077, 078, 217, 222, 230, 231, 346, 352, 355, 493,
496, 604, 609, 610

--- Pablo Correa - info@correapablo.com.ar
229, 357, 494, 497, 498, 501

--- Philippe Tempelman - philippe@superdesign2000.com
080, 234

--- Rejane Dal Bello - rejane@dalbello.com.br
073, 081, 082, 083, 084, 085, 086, 087

Directory
by number

001 - Accentuate - johnny@accentuateclothing.com
002 - Accentuate - johnny@accentuateclothing.com
003 - Akafab - stuff@akafab.com
004 - Akafab - stuff@akafab.com
005 - Artur Kja - guerrilha.ct@gmail.com
006 - Bettino - beto@beto-caracas.jazztel.es
007 - Rogerio Lionzo - rogeriolionzo@gmail.com
008 - Artur Kja - guerrilha.ct@gmail.com
009 - Artur Kja - guerrilha.ct@gmail.com
010 - Artur Kja - guerrilha.ct@gmail.com
011 - Artur Kja - guerrilha.ct@gmail.com
012 - Artur Kja - guerrilha.ct@gmail.com
013 - Artur Kja - guerrilha.ct@gmail.com
014 - Distrito Zero - 3ttman@distritozero.com
015 - Atnic - nina@stalina.de
016 - Bonus T-Shirts - renatojapi@hotmail.com
017 - Bonus T-Shirts - renatojapi@hotmail.com
018 - Bonus T-Shirts - renatojapi@hotmail.com
019 - Bonus T-Shirts - renatojapi@hotmail.com
020 - Eduardo Duccigne - eduardo@ilusorium.net
021 - Bonus T-Shirts - renatojapi@hotmail.com
022 - Bonus T-Shirts - renatojapi@hotmail.com
023 - Booware - us@boohome.com
024 - Booware - us@boohome.com
025 - David Steel - info@whoisdavidsteel.com
026 - Eduardo Duccigne - eduardo@ilusorium.net
027 - David Steel - info@whoisdavidsteel.com
028 - David Steel - info@whoisdavidsteel.com
029 - Embassy - victor@aurabarcelona.com
030 - Embassy - victor@aurabarcelona.com
031 - Endlessway - nikita@entity.ee
032 - Hugo Mulder - dhm@euronet.nl
033 - Embassy - victor@aurabarcelona.com
034 - Embassy - victor@aurabarcelona.com
035 - Hugo Mulder - dhm@euronet.nl
036 - Hugo Mulder - dhm@euronet.nl
037 - Guilherme Marconi - marconi@cloning.com.br
038 - Guilherme Marconi - marconi@cloning.com.br
039 - Fidalgo - contato@marcioismail.com.br

```
119 - Artur Kja - guerrilha.ct@gmail.com
120 - Artur Kja - guerrilha.ct@gmail.com
121 - Artur Kja - guerrilha.ct@gmail.com
122 - Artur Kja - guerrilha.ct@gmail.com
123 - Artur Kja - guerrilha.ct@gmail.com
124 - Artur Kja - guerrilha.ct@gmail.com
125 - Artur Kja - guerrilha.ct@gmail.com
126 - Artur Kja - guerrilha.ct@gmail.com
127 - Augusto Reis - contact@dside.com.br
128 - Artur Kja - guerrilha.ct@gmail.com
129 - Atypyk - contact@atypyk.com
130 - Atypyk - contact@atypyk.com
131 - Atypyk - contact@atypyk.com
132 - Augusto Reis - contact@dside.com.br
133 - Bettino - beto@beto-caracas.jazztel.es
134 - Atypyk - contact@atypyk.com
135 - Atypyk - contact@atypyk.com
136 - Atypyk - contact@atypyk.com
137 - Atypyk - contact@atypyk.com
138 - Bettino - beto@beto-caracas.jazztel.es
139 - Bettino - beto@beto-caracas.jazztel.es
140 - Atypyk - contact@atypyk.com
141 - Atypyk - contact@atypyk com
142 - Atypyk - contact@atypyk.com
143 - Atypyk - contact@atypyk.com
144 - Bettino - beto@beto-caracas.jazztel.es
145 - Bettino - beto@beto-caracas.jazztel.es
146 - Atypyk - contact@atypyk.com
147 - Bettino - beto@beto-caracas.jazztel.es
148 - Bettino - beto@beto-caracas.jazztel.es
149 - Bettino - beto@beto-caracas.jazztel.es
150 - Bettino - beto@beto-caracas.jazztel.es
151 - Bettino - beto@beto-caracas.jazztel.es
152 - Bettino - beto@beto-caracas.jazztel.es
153 - Bettino - beto@beto-caracas.jazztel.es
154 - Bonus T-Shirts - renatojapi@hotmail.com
155 - Bonus T-Shirts - renatojapi@hotmail.com
156 - Camiseteria - info@camiseteria.com.br
157 - Camiseteria - info@camiseteria.com.br
158 - Dale Murray - dale@itchcom.com
```

159 - Dale Murray - dale@itchcom.com
160 - Dale Murray - dale@itchcom.com
161 - Dale Murray - dale@itchcom.com
162 - Dale Murray - dale@itchcom.com
163 - Destroy Clothing - adam@destroyclothing.com
164 - Destroy Clothing - adam@destroyclothing.com
165 - Fidalgo - contato@marcioismail.com.br
166 - Eduardo Duccigne - eduardo@ilusorium.net
167 - Eduardo Duccigne - eduardo@ilusorium.net
168 - Femur - info@femur.com.br
169 - Femur - info@femur.com.br
170 - Femur - info@femur.com.br
171 - Fidalgo - contato@marcioismail.com.br
172 - Headstrong - info@headstrong.co.uk
173 - Garus Booth - bythebooth@bythebooth.com
174 - Garus Booth - bythebooth@bythebooth.com
175 - Garus Booth - bythebooth@bythebooth.com
176 - Goodforhealth - info@goodforhealth.tk
177 - Guilherme Marconi - marconi@cloning.com.br
178 - Headstrong - info@headstrong.co.uk
179 - Guilherme Marconi - marconi@cloning.com.br
180 - Haroldo Portella - hportela@iis.com.br
181 - Guilherme Marconi - marconi@cloning.com.br
182 - Guilherme Marconi - marconi@cloning.com.br
183 - Headstrong - info@headstrong.co.uk
184 - Headstrong - info@headstrong.co.uk
185 - Hayato Kamono - hayatok@designurge.com
186 - Headstrong - info@headstrong.co.uk
187 - Lalacompany - info@lalacompany.com
188 - Lalacompany - info@lalacompany.com
189 - Jaguar Negro - info@jaguar-negro.com
190 - Lowriderteeshirt - shop@lowriderteeshirt.ch
191 - Lars Niebuhr - lars@dcidenow.com
192 - Lars Niebuhr - lars@dcidenow.com
193 - Lars Niebuhr - lars@dcidenow.com
194 - Lars Niebuhr - lars@dcidenow.com
195 - Lowriderteeshirt - shop@lowriderteeshirt.ch
196 - Luciano Cian Van Der Durke - cian@hiatofc.com.br
197 - Lars Niebuhr - lars@dcidenow.com
198 - Lars Niebuhr - lars@dcidenow.com

397 - Artur Kja - guerrilha.ct@gmail.com
398 - Artur Kja - guerrilha.ct@gmail.com
399 - Artur Kja - guerrilha.ct@gmail.com
400 - Artur Kja - guerrilha.ct@gmail.com
401 - Augusto Reis - contact@dside.com.br
402 - Artur Kja - guerrilha.ct@gmail.com
403 - Artur Kja - guerrilha.ct@gmail.com
404 - Augusto Reis - contact@dside.com.br
405 - Balcony-ppl - visualmorphers@yahoo.com
406 - Bettino - beto@beto-caracas.jazztel.es
407 - Camiseteria - info@camiseteria.com.br
408 - Camiseteria - info@camiseteria.com.br
409 - Balcony-ppl - visualmorphers@yahoo.com
410 - Balcony-ppl - visualmorphers@yahoo.com
411 - David Steel - info@whoisdavidsteel.com
412 - Camiseteria - info@camiseteria.com.br
413 - Camiseteria - info@camiseteria.com.br
414 - Dale Murray - dale@itchcom.com
415 - David Steel - info@whoisdavidsteel.com
416 - Destroy Clothing - adam@destroyclothing.com
417 - Augusto Reis - contact@dside.com.br
418 - Embassy - victor@aurabarcelona.com
419 - Destroy Clothing - adam@destroyclothing.com
420 - Destroy Clothing - adam@destroyclothing.com
421 - Destroy Clothing - adam@destroyclothing.com
422 - Destroy Clothing - adam@destroyclothing.com
423 - Distrito Zero - 3ttman@distritozero.com
424 - Embassy - victor@aurabarcelona.com
425 - Destroy Clothing - adam@destroyclothing.com
426 - Destroy Clothing - adam@destroyclothing.com
427 - Destroy Clothing - adam@destroyclothing.com
428 - Eduardo Duccigne - eduardo@ilusorium.net
429 - Eduardo Duccigne - eduardo@ilusorium.net
430 - Embassy - victor@aurabarcelona.com
431 - Gary Gao - angrytoast@gmail.com
432 - Embassy - victor@aurabarcelona.com
433 - Fabio Nakane - fnakane@yahoo.com.br
434 - Fabio Nakane - fnakane@yahoo.com.br
435 - Fabio Nakane - fnakane@yahoo.com.br
436 - Femur - info@femur.com.br

437 - Edward Stuart - e_c_stuart@hotmail.com
438 - Femur - info@femur.com.br
439 - Gary Gao - angrytoast@gmail.com
440 - Guilherme Marconi - marconi@cloning.com.br
441 - Femur - info@femur.com.br
442 - Guilherme Marconi - marconi@cloning.com.br
443 - Guilherme Marconi - marconi@cloning.com.br
444 - Guilherme Marconi - marconi@cloning.com.br
445 - Guilherme Marconi - marconi@cloning.com.br
446 - Guilherme Marconi - marconi@cloning.com.br
447 - Guilherme Marconi - marconi@cloning.com.br
448 - Guilherme Marconi - marconi@cloning.com.br
449 - Guilherme Marconi - marconi@cloning.com.br
450 - Harderthansatan - info@harderthansatan.com
451 - Harderthansatan - info@harderthansatan.com
452 - Haroldo Portella - hportela@iis.com.br
453 - Guilherme Marconi - marconi@cloning.com.br
454 - Guilherme Marconi - marconi@cloning.com.br
455 - Haroldo Portella - hportela@iis.com.br
456 - Haroldo Portella - hportela@iis.com.br
457 - Hayato Kamono - hayatok@designurge.com
458 - Hayato Kamono - hayatok@designurge.com
459 - Guilherme Marconi - marconi@cloning.com.br
460 - Guilherme Marconi - marconi@cloning.com.br
461 - Headstrong - info@headstrong.co.uk
462 - Headstrong - info@headstrong.co.uk
463 - Hugo Mulder - dhm@euronet.nl
464 - Headstrong - info@headstrong.co.uk
465 - Headstrong - info@headstrong.co.uk
466 - Headstrong - info@headstrong.co.uk
467 - Hugo Mulder - dhm@euronet.nl
468 - Hugo Mulder - dhm@euronet.nl
469 - Headstrong - info@headstrong.co.uk
470 - Jason Byron Nelson - info@jasonbyronnelson.com

www.accentuateclothing.com
www.bonustshirts.com.br
www.camiseteria.com
www.cult.co.uk
www.digitalgravel.com
www.dside.com.br
www.headstrong.co.uk
www.krudmart.com
www.mutualresponse.com
www.spunky.co.uk
www.threadless.com
www.urbanindustry.co.uk
www.usc.co.uk

Websites

This book is dedicated to my son Diego

I am very grateful to all people who have participated in this book.
I would like to thank all the designers and graphic studios who have
collaborated on this book.

Without these people, this project would not have been possible:
Adriana Jordan, Antoni Canal, Isabel Lorente and Pamela Santacroce

Brunno Gens

Cati Fernandez

Daniel Japiassú "DJ"

Guilherme Dutra "Gaúcho"

Henrique Guitton

João Guitton

Júlia Camargo

Leandro Camargo "The Big"

Marcelo Machado "Chipa"

Myrla Guitton

Rodrigo Sampaio "Didi"

StÈsio Henri Guitton

Teresa Guitton

Accentuate Clothing - Johnny Quach

Bettino - Albert Carreras

Bonus T-Shirts - Renato Japiassú "Japi"

By the Booth - Garus Booth

Head Strong - Glyn Berrington

Mutual Response - Dofl Y. H. Yu

Adriana Jordan

Graduated in Marketing, Master in Positioning/Branding. Currently working on a PhD in Administration at the Universitat Politècnica de Catalunya (Technical University of Catalonia), Spain.

She has 7 years of experience working in important marketing and fashion companies in Rio de Janeiro, California and Barcelona. Now she is working as the coordinator of the courses taught in English (fashion marketing, advertising and interior design) at the IED, Istituto Europeo di Design (European Institute of Design).

She believes that traveling and learning about new cultures is the best way to enjoy life!
www.adrianajordan.com

Pedro Guitton

A Brazilian-born Spanish citizen. Graphic designer with an MBA in Marketing, currently doing a PhD in "Personal Branding".

He teaches at the IED - Istituto Europeo di Design (European Institute of Design), is the author of the books Marca 2000, Logos do Brasil and Logos from North to South America, and has given talks on corporate identity throughout the world.

His graphic influences come from a mix of experiences acquired in the places he where has lived, worked and studied: Rio de Janeiro (happiness and beauty), California (style and dream) and Barcelona, his current city (art and history).
www.pedroguitton.com